Questions AND Answers

INVENTIONS

Wendy Madgwick

KINGFISHER

KINGFISHER
Kingfisher Publications Plc
New Penderel House
283-288 High Holborn
London WC1V 7HZ
www.kingfisherpub.com

First published by Kingfisher Publications Plc in 2000
10 9 8 7 6 5 4 3

3TR/0501/TIM/HBM/130MA

Copyright © Kingfisher Publications Plc 2000

ISBN 0 7534 0481 8

Printed in China

Author: Wendy Madgwick
Designed, edited and typeset: Tucker Slingsby Ltd

Illustrations:
Susanna Addario, Marion Appleton, Julian Baker, Owain Bell, Simone Boni, Peter
Bull, John Burgess, Vanessa Card, Kuo Kang Chen, Richard Draper, Chris Forsey,
Terry Gabbey, Jeremy Gower, Ruby Green, Nick Harris, Adam Hook, Biz Hull,
Roger Kent, Chris Lyons, Kevin Maddison, Janos Marffy, Nicki Palin, Alex Pang,
Mike Roffe, Mike Saunders, Guy Smith, Tony Smith, Mark Stacey, Ian Thompson

Picture credits:
cover and p. 3 tl Nokia; p. 5 br Science Photo Library; p. 7 c Science Photo
Library/Mehau Kulyk; p. 27 cl Nokia; p. 29 bl Mary Evans Picture Library

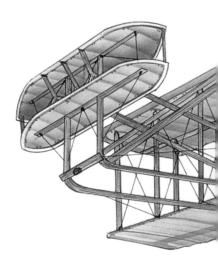

Contents

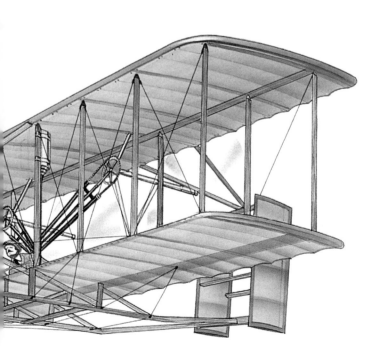

Writing and Printing	4
Medicine	6
Buildings	8
Food and Agriculture	10
At Home	12
Clothes and Fabrics	14
Useful Materials	16
Toys and Games	18
Energy	20
Calculations	22
Computers	24
Communication	26
On Film	28
Travel on Land	30
On the Sea	32
By Air	34
Into Space	36
Timeline	38
Index	40

Writing and Printing

The first true writing system was invented by the Sumerians over 5,000 years ago. They used pictures called pictograms to stand for objects, ideas and sounds. Today, the written or printed word is central to human communication.

Who invented printing?

Block printing was invented by the Chinese nearly 2,000 years ago. They carved characters on wooden blocks, covered them in ink and stamped them on to paper. Modern printing, with movable metal type, began in the 1440s when a German, Johannes Gutenberg, developed the printing press.

When were full stops and commas first used?

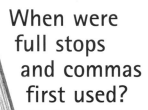

Medieval monks and scribes produced handwritten, beautifully decorated illuminated manuscripts. To make the manuscripts easier to read, the scribes separated words with spaces, used capital and small letters and introduced a system of punctuation, including full stops and commas.

Why did typewriters make you crazy?

People are often scared of a new inventions. When the first typewriter went on sale in 1874, some doctors said that using one could make you go mad! However, the typewriter was a huge success for its American inventor, Christopher Latham Sholes. The first successful portable typewriter appeared in the early 1900s and electric typewriters whizzed into action in 1901.

Who invented the paper clip?

The paper clip is such a simple and useful design, it is surprising that it is quite a recent invention. It first appeared in 1900, invented by Johan Vaalar, a young scientist who worked for an invention office in Norway. Before the paper clip, people used straight pins or ribbons tied through holes in the corner of the pages to fasten papers together temporarily.

Who was Mr Biro?

Ladislao Biro, a Hungarian journalist, invented the ballpoint pen in 1938. It contained a tube of quick-drying ink which rolled evenly on to the paper thanks to a tiny movable ball at the tip.

What was the first advertisement?

The oldest known piece of publicity is an ancient Egyptian papyrus dating from almost 5,000 years ago. The message is written in hieroglyphs, or picture writing, and offers a reward for finding a runaway slave.

Is there really lead in a pencil?

No! The 'lead' in a pencil is not made from the metal lead at all. It's made from graphite mixed with clay. The modern pencil was invented independently by Frenchman Nicholas-Jacque Conte and Austrian Josef Hardtmuth in 1795. Their invention was a great success – it could be easily sharpened and erased.

How does a mouse draw?

A computer mouse allows you to direct the cursor around the screen to give the computer commands. Using a mouse, designers can draw new details on to a picture. The computer mouse was invented in the United States in 1964 by Douglas Englehart. He also invented a foot-controlled 'rat' but it never caught on.

Why were felt-tip pens invented?

The Japanese inventor hoped that the pen's soft tip would make people's handwriting more graceful – like the brushstrokes in Japanese writing. The first felt-tips went on sale in Japan in 1962.

Medicine

Doctors in the ancient world used herbs, surgery and 'magic' to treat illnesses. Scientific medicine began in the 1600s with the invention of the microscope and an understanding of anatomy. Technical advances in the 1900s led to modern medicine.

Who were the first doctors?

The earliest doctors were physicians in ancient Egypt and China. In Egypt, physicians used drugs and potions. Surgeons treated injuries, and priests dealt with evil spirits. The first known physician was an Egyptian, Imhotep, who lived about 4,600 years ago.

When were bacteria discovered?

The Dutch instrument-maker Antonie van Leeuwenhoek made the first high-powered microscope. It could magnify up to 200 times. In 1683, he published drawings of bacteria – tiny living things that can cause disease. He was building on the work of English scientist Robert Hooke who, 20 years before, had discovered that living things were made up of small cells.

Modern microscope

Who discovered how blood flows?

In 1628, an English doctor, William Harvey, found that the heart pumps blood into the arteries. He showed that it circulates all around the body and returns to the heart along the veins.

Are drugs made from plants?

Most modern drugs are made from chemicals, but many were originally made from plants. For example, the heart drug, digitalis, comes from foxgloves. Quinine from the cinchona tree is used to treat malaria and aspirin is made from the bark of the willow.

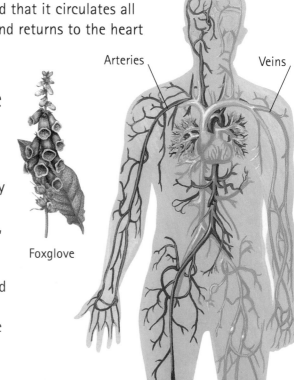

Foxglove

Arteries

Veins

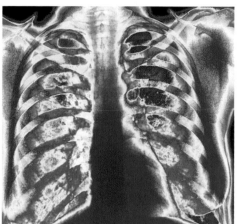

Artificial arm and hand

Prosthetic hook

Can artificial limbs move?

Back in the Middle Ages, the French surgeon Amboise Paré used springs and cogs to move artificial arms and legs. Today, whole legs and arms can be replaced with computer-controlled plastic or metal limbs. In some cases, nerve-endings in the patient's limb send messages to motors in the artificial limb to make it move.

How can we 'see' our bones?

We can see the bones in our bodies by taking X-rays of them. In 1895, the German scientist Wilhelm Röntgen first discovered that X-rays could pass through paper, wood and flesh, but not through metal or bone. Within months, doctors were using X-rays to photograph bones in the body.

What is a body scan?

In 1972, British scientist Godfrey Hounsfield developed a Computerized Tomography (CT) scanner to take pictures of the inside of the body. CT scanners take thousands of X-rays of the brain and body and build them up into a kind of 3-D picture for doctors to study.

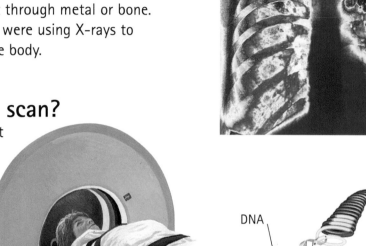

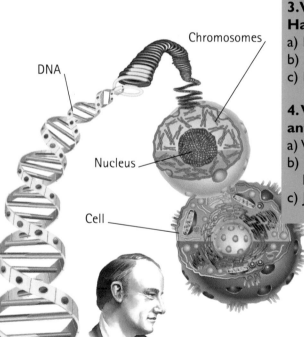

DNA

Chromosomes

Nucleus

Cell

Francis Crick

James Watson

Who made surgery safer?

In 1865, the Scottish surgeon Joseph Lister was the first doctor to use antiseptics during surgery to stop patients dying from infections. He sprayed carbolic acid round the operating theatre and soaked dressings in it to kill germs.

Early carbolic acid spray

What is the double helix?

DNA (deoxyribonucleic acid) is the chemical that controls how cells behave and reproduce. In 1953, two scientists Francis Crick from England and the American James Watson worked out that DNA was made up of a twisted spiral — a double helix.

Buildings

The first permanent buildings were put up about 10,000 years ago. At first people used natural materials, such as wood and stone, and most of the work was done by hand with simple tools. Today, hi-tech machines and the latest materials are used to build huge skyscrapers.

What is a Gothic building?

The Gothic style of building began in the mid-1100s in western Europe. It was mainly used for churches and cathedrals, which often had tall spires and towers, pointed arches, carved stonework and fancy windows. The workers had to scramble up and down wooden scaffolding tied up with rope, as there were no cranes to help them.

What was Stonehenge for?

Stonehenge, England, was built about 5,000 years ago. The standing megaliths (big stones) were arranged to mark the midsummer sunrise and the midwinter moonrise. It may have been a religious meeting place or a huge outdoor calendar used to study the movement of the Sun.

Can bridges carry water?

Bridges for carrying water were first built by the Assyrians, around 700 BC. Three hundred years later, the Romans improved the technique and built huge stone aqueducts to supply their cities with running water. Many Roman aqueducts still stand today.

Who designed a sail-like roof?

One of the most stunning modern buildings is the Opera House in Sydney Harbour, Australia. The architect, Jorn Utzon from Denmark, designed it to look like wind-filled sails. The main roof was made from concrete segments covered with thousands of ceramic tiles. The Opera House took 15 years to build. It was finished in 1973.

How old are the pyramids?

The first true pyramid was built in Egypt in about 2575 BC. Each of these huge tombs for the dead pharaohs took about 20 years to build. Thousands of workers dragged the huge stones up ramps and levered them into place with wooden poles.

Are there wire bridges?

In 1883, the Brooklyn Bridge in New York, United States, was the first suspension bridge built using steel cables, which can carry huge loads. Its designer, John Roebling, used over 1,900 kilometres of wire anchored with around 90,000 tonnes of masonry.

How are suspension bridges built?

The towers are built first. Steel ropes are suspended from the towers. Special machines spin these into strong steel cables. Next, long steel cables called hangers are attached to the suspending cables. Sections of the deck are lifted into place and fixed to the hangers.

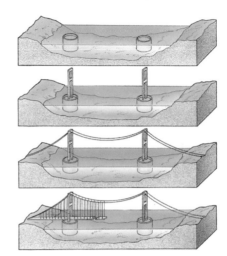

Quick-fire Quiz

1. Who invented aqueducts?
a) The Romans
b) The Greeks
c) The Assyrians

2. When did the Brooklyn Bridge open?
a) 1783
b) 1883
c) 1983

3. What was a pyramid?
a) A royal palace
b) A royal tomb
c) A royal throne

4. What is a megalith?
a) A big building
b) A big bridge
c) A big stone

Do buildings have skeletons?

In the 1880s, architects had the idea of using a skeleton of steel and concrete columns to support the roof, walls and floors of tall buildings. They fixed the outer walls to this framework. The first skyscraper, built in Chicago in the United States, was ten storeys tall. Today many tower over 400 metres high.

Food and Agriculture

Farming probably began about 10,000 years ago in the Middle East. Early farmers harvested wild wheat and barley and sowed some of the seeds to grow new crops. Gradually, farmers developed tools and, after the 1700s, farms began to be mechanised.

Did early farmers use ploughs?

Wooden ploughs developed from digging sticks used in Mesopotamia over 5,500 years ago. At first, people pulled ploughs, but then oxen were used. Ploughs with iron blades to break up heavy soil were made about 4,000 years later. More land could be cultivated with these, so farms grew larger.

Who first used windmills?

Windmills were first used in Persia over 1,200 years ago. By the 1200s they were being used in Europe, mainly to grind grain. During the 1700s and 1800s thousands were built to grind grain, power saws, raise materials from mines and pump water.

What is a combine harvester?

A combine harvester reaps, threshes, loads grain on to trailers and bales the leftover straw. The first one, built by an American, Hyram Moore, in the late 1830s, was pulled by horses. Later, tractors were used. By the 1930s, they were diesel-powered.

Who invented the milking machine?

In 1860, American Lee Colvin had an idea to speed up milking. Hoses linked rubber caps on the cow's teats to a bucket and bellows. Pumping the bellows milked the cow. Modern milking machines use a similar idea. Today, many milking parlours are computer-controlled.

Cups fit over a cow's teats

What is organic farming?

Artificial fertilizers were first made commercially by Sir John Bennet Lawes in England in 1842. Now many farmers use them to increase crop yields. In the 1970s, some farmers, worried about the effects of these fertilizers, returned to organic farming, in which only natural fertilizers are used.

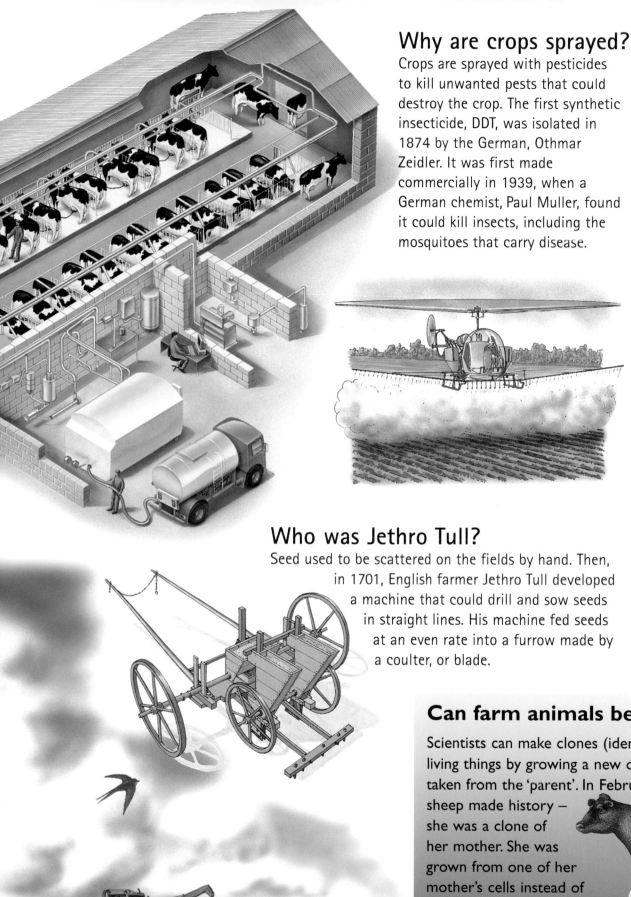

Why are crops sprayed?

Crops are sprayed with pesticides to kill unwanted pests that could destroy the crop. The first synthetic insecticide, DDT, was isolated in 1874 by the German, Othmar Zeidler. It was first made commercially in 1939, when a German chemist, Paul Muller, found it could kill insects, including the mosquitoes that carry disease.

Who was Jethro Tull?

Seed used to be scattered on the fields by hand. Then, in 1701, English farmer Jethro Tull developed a machine that could drill and sow seeds in straight lines. His machine fed seeds at an even rate into a furrow made by a coulter, or blade.

Can farm animals be cloned?

Scientists can make clones (identical copies) of living things by growing a new organism from a cell taken from the 'parent'. In February 1997, Dolly the sheep made history — she was a clone of her mother. She was grown from one of her mother's cells instead of from an egg. A year later, a cow was produced in the same way.

At Home

The first homes were caves and simple huts. Slowly, people developed new skills to build better homes, preserve food and make their lives more comfortable. Modern homes have electricity, gas, water and drainage and lots of household goods and furniture.

Prehistoric home

Waste ti

Well

Open fire

Preserved fish

Central heating radiator

Sewerage pipe

Water pipe

Have homes changed?

In prehistoric times (and in some parts of the world today) people lived in homes built from mud or stones, cooked on open fires and got water from wells. Modern homes are stronger and more comfortable.
From the 1880s homes were wired with electricity, giving light and power at the flick of a switch.

Who invented furniture?

Simple wooden furniture has probably been around since people began to build permanent homes. In Egypt, beautiful carved furniture was being made over 3,500 years ago. These luxurious articles were found in a tomb for a dead pharaoh to use in the afterlife.

When did irons 'go electric'?

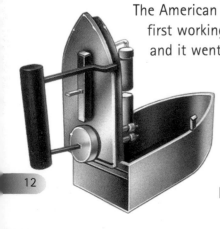

The American Henry Seely made the first working electric iron in 1882 and it went on sale in 1885. Before that, people used 'flat irons'. These were solid metal irons that had to be heated up on a fire before they could be used to press their clothes.

How was food kept cool?

Over 4,000 years ago, people stored food in ice pits to keep it cool. Early domestic refrigerators – insulated cabinets for holding ice – first appeared in the United States around 1850. The first mechanical one, powered by a steam pump, was the bright idea of German engineer Karl von Linde in 1879. Within 12 years he had sold 12,000 in Germany and the United States. The first electrical refrigerator, developed by Swedish engineers von Platen and Munters, went on sale in 1925.

How old is the flushing toilet?

Over 5,000 years ago, the Mesopotamians had special seats with holes and water running underneath to take away the waste. This idea was developed further by the English inventor John Harington, who published the earliest design for a flushing toilet with a cistern in 1596. The first practical flushing toilet was made by Alexander Cumming in the 1770s.

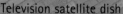
Modern home

Television satellite dish

Electrical power

Chamber pot

Flushing toilet

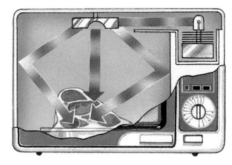

Which waves can melt chocolate?

American Percy Spencer discovered microwave cooking by accident. He'd been working on ways of using invisible microwaves to detect aircraft. When he found that these waves had melted a chocolate bar in his pocket, he realised they could be used to cook food too. In 1946, the first microwave oven was developed and in 1955, commercial ones appeared.

How old is central heating?

The ancient Romans first developed a method of heating their houses with hot air nearly 2,000 years ago. Called a hypocaust , warm air, heated by burning fuel in a furnace, flowed through tiled flues in the walls into the spaces beneath the floor, heating the rooms above.

Who lit up homes?

In 1878, the Briton Joseph Swan demonstrated his electric light bulb. A year later, the American inventor Thomas Edison made a long-lasting light bulb with a carbon filament, which went on sale in 1880. The two men eventually set up a joint company to make light bulbs.

Clothes and Fabrics

Early people wore animal skins to keep them warm, but about 10,000 years ago people learned how to make cloth. They used a spindle to spin wool, cotton, flax or hemp into thread, which could be woven into fabric. These fabrics were then made into clothes.

How old are needles?

Bone needles over 20,000 years old were found in Stone Age caves in France. They were probably used to stitch animal skins together. Modern metal needles were not developed until the 1400s.

How do zips work?

Zips have two rows of teeth joined together by a sliding 'key' which locks the teeth together or pulls them apart. The American Whitcomb Judson invented the first zip fasteners in the 1890s. In 1913, Gideon Sundback patented the interlocking zip fastener.

Who wore safety pins?

Ancient Egyptians first invented safety-pin type clasps which they wore like brooches. The modern safety pin was 're-invented' by American Walter Hunt in 1849. He didn't make any money from his invention – he gave the patent away to repay a $15 debt!

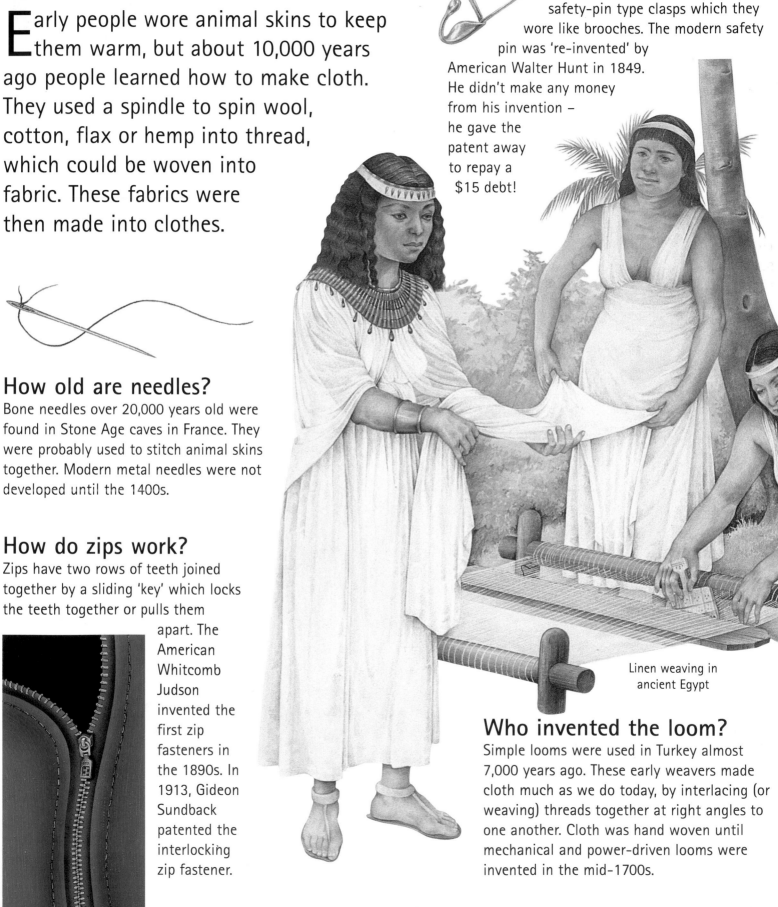

Linen weaving in ancient Egypt

Who invented the loom?

Simple looms were used in Turkey almost 7,000 years ago. These early weavers made cloth much as we do today, by interlacing (or weaving) threads together at right angles to one another. Cloth was hand woven until mechanical and power-driven looms were invented in the mid-1700s.

Are shoes made in factories?

Shoes have been around for thousands of years and, until the mid-1800s, they were all handmade. These Native American moccasins were made by hand from soft deer-skin and adorned with coloured porcupine quills. This took many hours. Today a pair of shoes can be made in minutes by a machine in a factory.

Quick-fire Quiz

1. When were zips invented?
a) 1690s
b) 1790s
c) 1890s

2. Who first made silk?
a) Romans
b) Native Americans
c) Chinese

3. Who invented the spinning jenny?
a) Whitcomb Judson
b) Elias Howe
c) James Hargreaves

4. What did George de Mestral make?
a) Velcro
b) Lock-stitch sewing machine
c) Safety pin

Which machine was destroyed?

French tailor Barthélemy Thimonnier developed a sewing machine in 1829. Other tailors destroyed it, fearing it would put them out of work. In the United States, a lock-stitch machine was invented by Walter Hunt in 1833 and Elias Howe made a better machine in 1845. Sewing machines became widely available in the late 1850s.

Early sewing machine

Who tanned leather?

Leather clothing, footwear and household goods were used over 5,000 years ago in Mesopotamia. In the past, people 'tanned' leather by rubbing the hides with the juices of bark and roots that contain the chemical tannin. (This is where 'tanning' gets its name.) Sometimes skins were soaked in salt and the chemical alum to preserve them.

What was a spinning jenny?

In 1764, Englishman James Hargreaves invented an automatic spinning machine, the spinning jenny. It could spin eight reels of thread at once, compared with the one reel made by an ordinary spinning wheel.

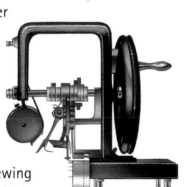

What was China's best-kept secret?

Silk was first discovered by the Chinese over 4,600 years ago. They set up farms to breed silk worms about 3,500 years ago but kept the method a secret for another 2,000 years. Silk was so valuable that the Chinese traded it for gold and silver.

What is Velcro?

Swiss engineer George de Mestral spent eight years developing Velcro. It is made from two nylon strips, one covered with tiny loops, the other with tiny hooks. The strips stick to each other when pressed together but can easily be ripped apart. Velcro went on sale in the mid-1960s.

Useful Materials

Once, people used natural materials such as wood or cotton to make things. Later, they discovered how to extract metals from ore found in the ground. Today, synthetic materials, such as nylon, plastic and fibreglass, are used to make many goods from cars to clothes.

Pottery-making in ancient China

Is glass made from sand?

Glass is made by heating silica (sand), limestone and soda to very high temperatures. It can then be coloured and shaped. Many medieval churches have windows made of stained glass, like this one. The oldest surviving window, in Augsberg Cathedral, Germany, dates from 1065.

Why do cars rust?

Iron and steel objects rust in damp air because the iron changes into a red-brown iron oxide, a mixture of iron and oxygen. In 1913, the Briton Harry Brearley added the metal chromium to steel to make the first successful rust-resistant stainless steel.

What is steel?

Steel, a strong metal made from iron, was first developed over 3,000 years ago. In 1856, the British inventor Henry Bessemer devised a cheap way of producing steel. Molten iron was poured into a converter and hot air or oxygen was blown over it. Most of the carbon in the iron was burned, turning it into steel.

Steel-making

Where was china made?

Pottery goods have been made for about 9,000 years, but fine china, or porcelain, was only invented about 1,200 years ago in China. The art remained a secret until just over 300 years ago, when fine porcelain goods were taken to the West.

Who first used plants to make materials?

People have made useful materials from plant fibres for thousands of years and many are still used today. About 5,000 years ago, cotton plants were first cultivated in India and the Chinese used the fibrous stems of hemp to make rope. The ancient Egyptians made fine linen fabric from flax stems.

Are plastics oily?

All plastics, such as polyvinylchloride (PVC), polythene, nylon and some paints, are made from chemicals found in oil, natural gas or coal. Polythene was first discovered by accident in 1933 by chemists working at ICI in Britain. Two years later, nylon was made by Wallace Carothers in the United States.

Is fibreglass strong?

Fibreglass material is made by mixing glass fibres and plastic. It was developed in the United States in the 1930s. It is flame-resistant, does not rust and is tough enough to make car bodies or boats. It is also used to insulate buildings.

Fibreglass canoe

What was Bakelite?

Bakelite radio

In 1909, a Belgian-American chemist named Leo Hendrik Baekeland made the world's first artificial plastic – Bakelite. As it did not conduct heat or electricity it was ideal for making electrical goods.

Is rubber liquid?

Natural rubber is made from the thick, runny sap, or latex, of rubber trees. The latex is collected, strained, mixed with acid to solidify it and rolled into sheets. Wild rubber was discovered in Brazil in the early 1800s and was first used for waterproofing. Today we mostly use synthetic rubbers, developed about 60 years ago.

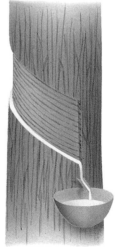

Toys and Games

Toys and games have been around for thousands of years. Some toys were just for fun, but many prepared children for adult life. Games also developed from the skills needed to hunt and fight. In some ancient cultures, sport was part of their religion.

How old is football?

No-one is sure when football began, but by the 1200s street football was a popular sport. There were no pitches, goals, or rules. The sole aim was to get the ball to your team's home ground. Men and boys chased the ball through the streets, knocking people out of their way. It got so rough that in 1314 King Edward II of England banned football in London.

When was chess invented?

Chess was invented about 1,400 years ago in India or China to help develop war skills. The board represents the field of battle and the pieces are different ranks and officers. The object of the game is to capture your opponent's king.

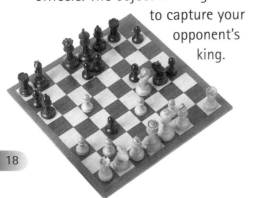

What's a home run?

In baseball, if the batter hits the ball and races round all four bases in one go, it's called a home run. Baseball developed in the United States in the 1800s from the British game of rounders. The first organized game was played in 1846.

When were jigsaws first made?

Jigsaws date back to the 1760s, when European map makers pasted maps on to wood and cut them up into pieces. These early wooden jigsaws did not interlock and were used for lessons rather than fun.

Who first played board games?

People first began to play board games around 4,000 years ago. This game from Mesopotamia dates from between 3000 and 2000 BC and is one of the oldest found. It has a marked board, dice and counters but no rules have survived, so no-one knows its name or how it was played.

Which captains lost their heads?

About 500 years ago, the Aztecs and Mayas of Central America played a ball game called tlochtli. The aim was to toss a rubber ball into the opposing team's end of the court, using only elbows, hips and knees. A team won outright if they hit the ball through a ring placed high up on the wall. The captain of the losing Aztec team was sometimes beheaded!

What is a Game Boy™?

In 1989, Nintendo of Japan launched their first hand-held video game – the Game Boy™. Even though the first games were very simple, the Game Boy™ was a huge success, selling over 100 million in four years. The first home video game – a simulated game of table tennis – was invented by the American Ralph Baer in 1972.

When was the first Olympic Games?

The first Games was a religious festival held in ancient Greece over 2,000 years ago. These ancient Games, held every four years, first featured just one race, but in time, with more contests, they lasted for five days. The modern Olympics date from 1896, and today over 7,000 athletes from 120 nations take part.

Which toy was named after an American president?

Teddy bears are named after the American president Theodore Roosevelt, called Teddy for short. Toy bears were the bright idea of a sweetshop owner who read a story about Roosevelt refusing to shoot a bear cub. He decided to stop selling sweets and make toy bears he called 'teddies' instead.

Energy

People use energy for all sorts of activities from powering cars to lighting their homes. Most of the energy we use is made by burning fossil fuels such as coal, gas and oil. Renewable energy sources such as solar, water and wind power can be used to generate electricity.

Arkwright's Mill

Did water-power run factories?

Watermills have been used for over 2,000 years to grind corn. In 1771, Richard Arkwright turned a watermill into a cloth-making factory, using the water wheel to power his new spinning machines.

What is a wind farm?

Modern windmills are used to turn machines called turbines which generate, or make, electricity. These wind turbines are grouped together in wind farms. The first large wind generator was built by the American Palmer Putnam in 1940.

Who made engines steam?

An English blacksmith, Thomas Newcomen, built the first practical steam engine in 1712. The Scotsman James Watt came up with an improved design and in 1782 his double-action steam engine was used to power factory machinery.

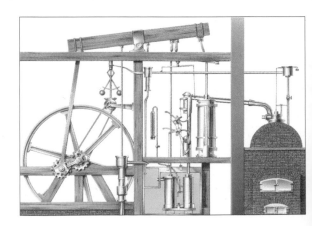

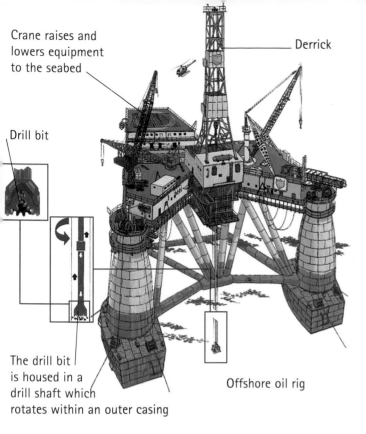

Crane raises and lowers equipment to the seabed

Derrick

Drill bit

The drill bit is housed in a drill shaft which rotates within an outer casing

Offshore oil rig

Is oil found under the sea?
In the 1970s, large oil deposits were found under the North Sea. Oil wells were drilled 200 metres beneath the sea. Offshore oil rigs had to be built to pump the oil to the surface. These rigs are supported on steel or concrete structures that are sunk deep into the seabed.

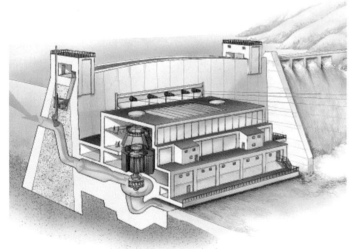

What is a hydrodam?
Hydroelectric power stations are often built inside dams called hydrodams. Water from a lake behind the dam gushes down pipes, turning turbines that drive generators and make electricity. The world's first major hydroelectric power station opened in 1895 at the Niagara Falls in North America.

Can the Sun heat a home?
A few modern homes have solar panels in the roof. Some use the Sun's heat to warm water. Others contain electronic devices called photovoltaic (solar) cells to change sunlight into electricity. Solar power can run machines. The first practical solar-powered machine, a steam engine, was developed by Frenchman Augustin Mouchet in 1861.

Who split the atom?
In 1932, British scientists John Cockroft and Ernest Walton first split the atom, releasing huge amounts of energy. In the United States, in 1942, Italian-born Enrico Fermi and his team built the first successful nuclear reactor to control this energy. In 1954, the first nuclear power station was opened in Russia.

What are fossil fuels?
Coal, oil and gas are called fossil fuels. Coal is the remains of ancient plants that lived and died in prehistoric forests. Oil and gas are made from the bodies of tiny dead sea creatures. The first coal-fired power station to generate electricity opened in 1882.

Quick-fire Quiz

1. When did the first nuclear power station open?
a) 1944
b) 1954
c) 1964

2. What did Fermi build?
a) Solar panels
b) A hydrodam
c) A nuclear reactor

3. Which of these is a fossil fuel?
a) Coal
b) Sunlight
c) Steam

4. Who built the first practical steam engine?
a) Mouchet
b) Arkwright
c) Newcomen

Calculations

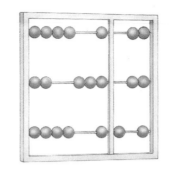
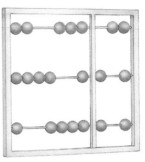

When people first began to count, they could get by using just fingers and toes. But soon they invented tally sticks and number systems to record and calculate measurements. Numbers are the basis of all calculations. Today, most people use a modern version of numbers invented in Arabia (0 to 10).

Who invented the abacus?

A simple abacus dates back to Mesopotamia, 5,000 years ago. The Chinese abacus, designed about 1,700 years ago, is made up of rows of beads representing units, tens, hundreds and thousands. It is a rapid tool for adding, subtracting, multiplying and dividing.

What was an astrolabe?

The astrolabe was originally a circular map of the heavens used by astronomers to measure the height of stars and planets. In the early Middle Ages, Arab scholars developed the astrolabe as an instrument to measure latitude and help them to navigate at sea.

Astrolabe

Moroccan students in the Middle Ages

What was the earliest money?

Long ago, people used to swap goods for the things they wanted. The people of ancient Lydia (now Turkey) were the first to make coins, about 2,700 years ago. They used electrum, a mixture of gold and silver. The Chinese invented paper bank notes about 1,200 years ago.

Who first used weights?

The first known standard weights and scales were used by the Babylonians about 4,600 years ago. The ancient Egyptians also used sensitive scales and weights to weigh precious stones and gold over 5,000 years ago.

The Babylonians used three standard weights.

22

Who made the first mechanical calculator?

The first mechanical calculator was made by the Frenchman Blaise Pascal in 1642 when he was aged only 19. It had a row of toothed wheels with numbers around them. Numbers to be added or subtracted were dialled in and the answer appeared behind holes at the top. Modern electronic pocket calculators went on sale in 1971. They can do complicated calculations in seconds.

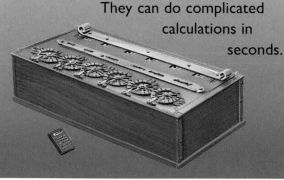

What was a handspan?

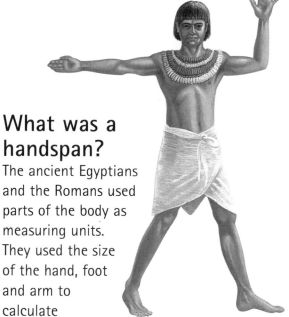

The ancient Egyptians and the Romans used parts of the body as measuring units. They used the size of the hand, foot and arm to calculate distances, but these measurements varied according to the size of the person making them. Eventually, standard measurements were adopted.

What were the first clocks?

Sundials and shadow clocks, which use the Sun's passage across the sky to measure time, were first used in ancient Egypt to tell the time. The Babylonians divided the sundial's circle into 360 parts or degrees and divided it into 12 hours. In the Middle Ages, the hour- or sandglass was a popular 'clock'. Atomic clocks were first developed in 1969 and are accurate to one second in 1.6 million years!

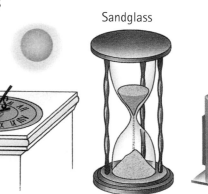

Atomic clock

Sandglass

Sundial

How do we measure temperature?

The first practical sealed alcohol thermometers, in which liquid rose up a tube as it heated, were made around 1660. In 1714, the German Gabriel Fahrenheit made a more accurate thermometer using mercury.

Alcohol thermometer

Who was Einstein?

Albert Einstein was a very clever German scientist who studied many things including energy and time. In 1915 he developed the theory of relativity, which says that time would slow down, length would shorten and mass would increase if you could travel almost as fast as the speed of light.

$E=mc^2$

Computers

Modern computers – electronic machines that can store and process masses of information – were first designed in the 1940s. Computers can do billions of calculations a second and we use them to carry out many tasks, from predicting the weather to making other machines.

What are microchips?

In the 1960s, scientists came up with a new way to run computers. They used a tiny slice, or chip, of a material called silicon to make the electronic 'brain' that controls a computer. Today a tiny microchip contains up to 250,000 parts that tell it how to work. A computer uses different microchips to do different jobs.

Who was Mr Babbage?

In 1834, the British mathematician Charles Babbage invented the first mechanical computer that could be programmed, but he did not have the money or technology to build it. His machine was finally made in 1991 – and it worked!

Why were computers as big as a room?

The Americans John Mauchly and J. Prosper Eckert Jr built the first proper automatic computer (ENIAC) in 1945. It filled two whole rooms and weighed as much as five elephants. It was this large because it used 19,000 valves, each as big as a hand, to control the switches that made it work. Computers got smaller in the 1950s when tiny transistors replaced valves.

Who developed PCs?

The first successful personal computer, or PC, was developed by Steve Jobs and Steve Wozniak in 1978. At first only a few people could afford them, but today personal computers are found in schools, offices and homes all over the world.

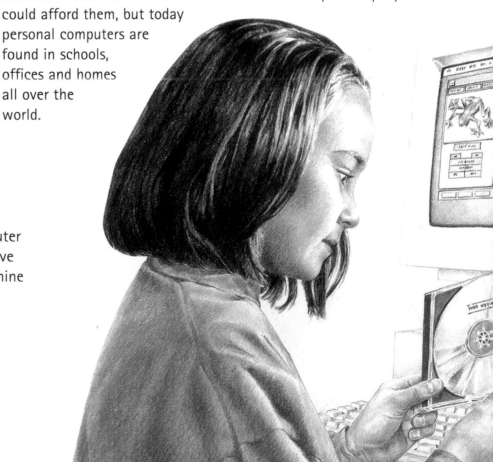

How do computers work?

All computers change the information they handle into numbers, which are stored as electrical signals. In modern computers these signals are either 'on', which stands for 1, or 'off', which stands for 0. All numbers, letters and pictures are turned into a sequence of 1s and 0s (called 'binary code'). A computer does rapid calculations using these numbers, which are then changed into words and pictures that you can understand.

Quick-fire Quiz

1. When was ENIAC built?
a) 1935
b) 1945
c) 1955

2. What are microchips made from?
a) Copper
b) Plastic
c) Silicon

3. What does PC stand for?
a) Personal computer
b) Private computer
c) Plastic computer

4. Who built a mechanical computer?
a) Eckert
b) Wozniak
c) Babbage

Do computers have disks?

The information used to run computer programs is usually stored as electrical pulses on magnetic disks. Plastic 'floppy disks' were created by the IBM company in 1970. In 1983, compact disks (CDs), plastic-coated metal disks read by laser, went on sale. CDs used by computers can store vast amounts of information.

Can robots see?

The first industrial robot – a computer-controlled machine that carries out tasks – was made in the United States in 1962. In 1980, the first robot that could 'see' using electronic eyes was developed in America. Today, some robots have laser vision systems and can both see and hear.

What is virtual reality?

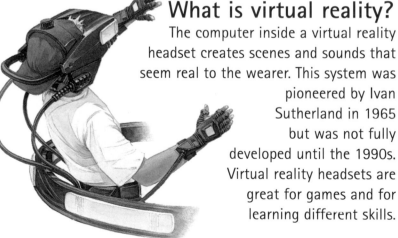

The computer inside a virtual reality headset creates scenes and sounds that seem real to the wearer. This system was pioneered by Ivan Sutherland in 1965 but was not fully developed until the 1990s. Virtual reality headsets are great for games and for learning different skills.

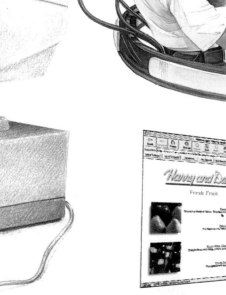

What is the Net?

Computers anywhere in the world can be linked via a telephone line and a gadget called a modem. This network, called the Internet or Net for short, is used by over 40 million people. The Internet was first developed in the late 1960s by the US government as a safe way to communicate in wartime.

Communications

Before the printing press was invented in the 1450s, people could only swap information by word of mouth or by writing letters. Today we use books, newspapers, radio, television, telephone and e-mail to spread news and views.

Who first recorded sound?

In 1877, the famous American inventor Thomas Edison built a machine to record sound. The sounds were stored as patterns of indented lines on a tin-foil cylinder. The first words to be recorded clearly were 'Mary had a little lamb'.

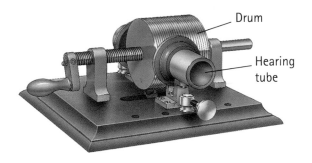

Drum

Hearing tube

Who rang the bell?

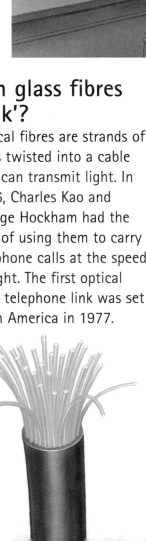

In 1875, the Scottish-American inventor Alexander Graham Bell discovered a way to send the human voice along wires. A year later he built the first working telephone and within months hundreds of telephone bells were ringing all over America.

Can glass fibres 'talk'?

Optical fibres are strands of glass twisted into a cable that can transmit light. In 1976, Charles Kao and George Hockham had the idea of using them to carry telephone calls at the speed of light. The first optical fibre telephone link was set up in America in 1977.

Who invented the radio?

The Italian Guglielmo Marconi built the first proper radio set that sent messages using radio waves in 1895. His machine produced radio waves by making a strong electric spark. The system was known as the wireless because the signals were sent through the air, not along a wire. Marconi sent the first signal across the Atlantic in 1901, and public radio broadcasts began about 20 years later.

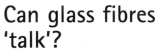

Who said 'number please'?

The first telephone exchange set up in America in 1878 was manual, with just 21 customers. An operator answered your call, took the number you wanted and plugged in your line to complete the electrical circuit and connect your call. The first automatic exchange was installed in America in 1892.

The Morse Code

a	•▬	s	•••
b	▬•••	t	▬
c	▬•▬•	u	••▬
d	▬••	v	•••▬
e	•	w	•▬▬
f	••▬•	x	▬••▬
g	▬▬•	y	▬•▬▬
h	••••	z	▬▬••
i	••	0	▬▬▬▬▬
j	•▬▬▬	1	•▬▬▬▬
k	▬•▬	2	••▬▬▬
l	•▬••	3	•••▬▬
m	▬▬	4	••••▬
n	▬•	5	•••••
o	▬▬▬	6	▬••••
p	•▬▬•	7	▬▬•••
q	▬▬•▬	8	▬▬▬••
r	•▬•	9	▬▬▬▬•

Early telegraph machine

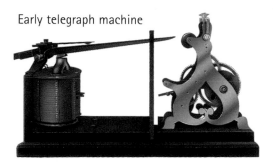

Quick-fire Quiz

1. What was *Telstar*?
a) A radio
b) A satellite
c) A phone

2. What did Marconi invent?
a) The telephone
b) The television
c) The radio

3. What are optical fibres made from?
a) Copper
b) Glass
c) Light

4. When was the telephone invented?
a) 1775
b) 1875
c) 1975

When did phones go mobile?

In the early 1980s, computers allowed the telephone to lose its wires and go mobile. A system of low-powered radio stations link the moving telephone to a computer network that keeps track of the caller.

What is Morse Code?

Before the telephone was invented people sent messages by telegraph. This used a coded series of short and long electrical signals – dots and dashes. It was invented by the American Samuel Morse.

How do telephone calls travel round the world?

Communication satellites orbiting the Earth pick up signals and send them on to a receiver thousands of kilometres away. *Telstar*, the first one, went into orbit in 1962. It could relay 12 telephone calls or one television channel. Satellites today carry thousands of calls and several channels at once.

On Film

Before cameras were developed people could only record images by drawing or painting them. Photography was invented in the early 1800s. At first it was a slow process and all pictures were in black and white. Now we have film and video cameras to record people and places all over the world.

Who first said 'Smile, please'?

The Frenchman Joseph Niépce took the first permanent photograph in about 1827. It took eight hours for the photo of a view to develop on a thin metal plate. In the late 1800s, taking photos was such a lengthy business that people needed a back rest to help them sit still!

What is a Polaroid®?

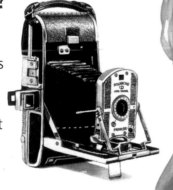

The Polaroid® camera, invented by the American Edwin Land in 1947, produces 'instant' photos. It uses slim plastic envelopes instead of a roll of film. Inside is a sheet of film and a packet of processing chemicals, which burst as the photo is ejected. The picture develops in about 60 seconds.

Did early cameras use rolls of film?

Early box cameras used a lens to focus the light rays on to a metal or glass photographic plate at the back of the camera. The light changed the chemicals on the plate and the picture developed in a few minutes. Rolls of film were first introduced in 1888 by the American George Eastman.

When did movie stars first talk?

Early movies were silent and actors had to be very good mime artists. Words came up on the screen to explain the action and an organist played mood music to liven up the film. The first full-length movie with sound was *The Jazz Singer*, shown in the United States in 1927. It was so popular that silent movies soon lost their appeal and 'talkies', talking pictures, took over.

Who invented television?

The Scottish inventor John Logie Baird first demonstrated the television in public in 1926. His original machine was made from an old box, knitting needles, a cake tin and a bicycle lamp! The first picture of a human face was a blurry image of 15-year-old William Taynton.

Rotating disc

Baird's television, 1930

Baird's camera had a mechanical scanner with a rotating disc. This was soon replaced by the electronic scanner developed by the American-Russian Vladimir Zworykin in 1923.

How do colour television cameras work?

The first colour televisions went on sale in the 1950s. Colour television cameras split the light from the scene being filmed into three images — one red, one green and one blue. The light from each image is turned into an electrical signal which is recorded with the sound signal on film or tape. A colour television converts these signals back into the coloured picture.

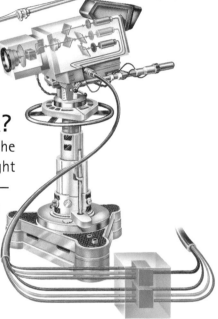

Who made the first movie?

The American Thomas Edison was the first person to film moving pictures, but the French brothers Auguste and Louis Lumière were the first to show a 'movie' to an audience. The brothers made 10 films in 1895 and built a machine to show them on screen to audiences in Paris clubs and cafés.

When did home videos arrive?

Videotape was invented in 1956 and the first camcorder, or video camera-recorder was developed in the 1960s. Modern lightweight camcorders went on sale in the 1980s. A camcorder uses magnetic tapes instead of photographic film to record the images and sound.

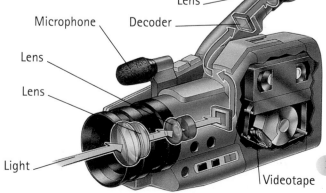

Lens

Microphone   Decoder

Lens

Lens

Light

Videotape

Travel on Land

Prehistoric people had to walk everywhere, carrying their goods or dragging them on sledges. By 3000 BC, people had developed wheeled vehicles pulled by animals. In the late 1800s, the invention of the steam engine and petrol engine changed land travel completely.

What is a TGV?

The French TGV, *Train à Grande Vitesse*, first went into service in 1981. These speedy electric trains can travel at over 300 kilometres an hour on special tracks. The first electric train was demonstrated at an exhibition in Germany in 1879.

Did cars run on steam?

The first cars ran on steam, but they were noisy and often broke down. Early cars were not allowed to travel faster than walking pace and in some countries a man with a red flag had to walk in front to warn people they were coming!

Who invented the wheel?

The wheel was invented about 5,500 years ago in the Middle East. It was laid on its side and used to make pottery. About 300 years later, the Sumerians living in the same region had turned wheels upright and were using them on horse-drawn chariots. The first wheels were solid, made from three planks of wood pegged together and cut to shape. The plank wheel turned on a fixed axle.

When was the bicycle invented?

The bicycle was invented in the 1790s in France, but you moved by pushing your feet along the ground! A German, Baron von Drais, made a bike with a steerable front wheel in 1817. The first bike with pedals and cranks to turn the back wheel was designed by the Scotsman Kirkpatrick Macmillan in 1839.

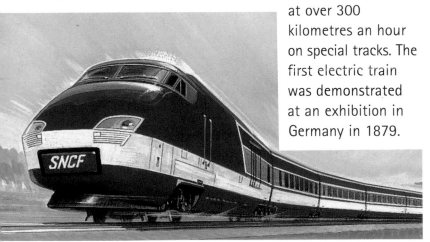

Can the Sun power cars?

Engineers are experimenting with a new form of energy to power car engines – energy from the Sun. Several prototypes run on solar-powered batteries. A few of these solar cars have reached speeds of 140 kilometres an hour in races across Australia.

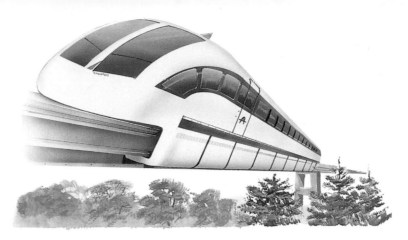

How do trains hover?

'Maglevs', or magnetic levitation trains, hover above the track supported by magnetic fields. The trains, driven by linear motors with no moving parts, can reach speeds of up to 700 kilometres an hour. These trains were pioneered in Germany and Japan in the 1980s.

Solar panels

Solar-powered car

Who was Mr Benz?

In 1885, the German engineer Karl Benz built the first vehicle to be powered by a petrol engine. The first true four-wheeled car was developed in 1886 by another German, Gottlieb Daimler.

Which train was a winner?

In 1829, Englishman George Stevenson and his son Robert entered a contest to find the fastest steam train. Their winning engine, the *Rocket*, could pull a train at 46 kilometres an hour – twice as fast as their rivals. The first steam locomotive was developed by the English engineer Richard Trevithick in 1803.

Quick-fire Quiz

1. What was a Tin Lizzie?
a) A train
b) A car
c) A bicycle

2. Who built the first petrol-powered vehicle?
a) Daimler
b) Benz
c) Ford

3. Who built the first steam train?
a) George Stevenson
b) Henry Ford
c) Richard Trevithick

4. How fast could the *Rocket* travel?
a) 56 km/h
b) 46 km/h
c) 36 km/h

What was a Tin Lizzie?

Hand-built early cars were too expensive for ordinary people. But in 1908, in America, Henry Ford had the idea of mass-producing cars on his other invention – the assembly line. In the next 20 years, he sold 15 million 'Model T' cars, also known as Tin Lizzies.

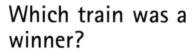

On the Sea

Early people travelled over water using rafts and dug-out canoes. About 5,000 years ago the Sumerians and Egyptians built ships with sails and oars. In the 1800s steam engines took over from sails and steel replaced wood. A hundred years later, ships with petrol engines took to the waves.

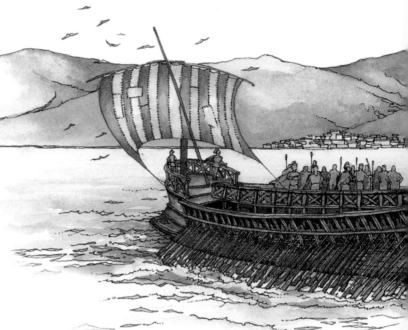

What was a trireme?

Triremes were fast galleys powered by three rows of oarsmen on each side. The Greeks first built triremes in about 650 BC. Later triremes were up to 40 metres long with a pointed ram at the front to smash into enemy ships.

When were paddle steamers first used?

The Frenchman Jouffroy d'Abbans built the first working steamboat in 1783. Within 20 years paddle steamers were being used to ferry people and goods up and down rivers and across the sea.

How did sailors find their way?

In the mid-1700s, two British inventions helped sailors fix their position at sea. The sextant, invented by John Campbell, determined latitude by measuring the angle of the Sun or stars above the horizon. John Harrison's chronometer – a kind of clock – helped to measure longitude.

Sextant

How do divers swim underwater?

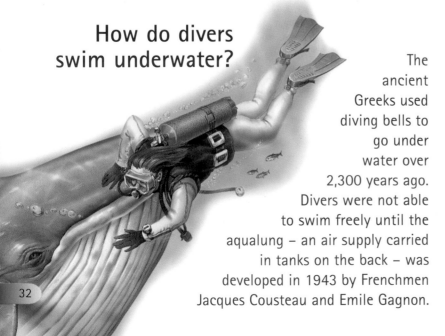

The ancient Greeks used diving bells to go under water over 2,300 years ago. Divers were not able to swim freely until the aqualung – an air supply carried in tanks on the back – was developed in 1943 by Frenchmen Jacques Cousteau and Emile Gagnon.

Why were clippers fast?

The super-fast clipper of the mid-1800s had a new shape of hull and a combination of square and triangular sails with which it could catch and use the slightest breeze. Clippers could maintain speeds of 37 kilometres an hour.

Quick-fire Quiz

1. When was the first steamboat trip?
   a) 1683
   b) 1783
   c) 1883

2. Who designed the hovercraft?
   a) Campbell
   b) Cockerel
   c) Gagnon

3. What was the *Turtle*?
   a) A steamship
   b) An aircraft carrier
   c) A submarine

4. Who first built triremes?
   a) Romans
   b) Egyptians
   c) Greeks

When were submarines invented?

In 1620, the Dutchman Cornelius Drebbel's wooden submarine, rowed by 12 oarsmen, travelled several kilometres up the River Thames in London, England. The *Turtle*, the first submarine that could rise and sink, was designed by the American David Bushnell in 1776. It was used in the American War of Independence.

The *Turtle*

What craft floats on air?

Hovercraft can skim over land or water on a cushion of air blown down by fans and trapped inside a flexible rubber skirt. The hovercraft was designed by the British engineer Christopher Cockerel in the 1950s and made its first test run in 1959.

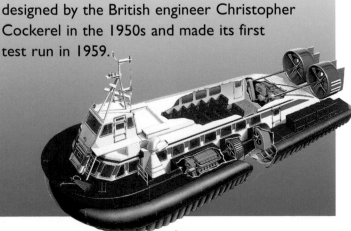

How do jet aircraft land on ships?

The first carrier for jet aircraft, *USS Forrestal*, was completed in 1955. Aircraft can take off and land on the deck in mid-ocean. During take-off the aircraft is propelled forward by a device called a 'catapult'. When it lands, the aircraft is slowed down by huge 'arrester' wires stretched across the deck.

By Air

Over 2,000 years ago the Chinese flew war kites to fire-bomb their enemies, but they did not travel in them. Air transport did not begin until the 1780s, when hot-air balloons took to the skies. Just over 100 years later, powered flight got off to a bumpy start.

How do hang-gliders fly?

Hang-gliders depend on the wind and rising warm air to fly. In 1853, British engineer George Cayley was the first to design a suitably shaped wing. Nearly 100 years later, in the 1940s, the American Francis Rogallo developed a triangular-shaped kite that gave rise to modern hang-gliders.

When was the first flight?

The first flight was made in a hot-air balloon on 21 November 1783 by François de Rozier and the Marquis d'Arlandes. The balloon, made by the French Montgolfier brothers, had a basket for passengers slung beneath the huge paper balloon.

Who was the first hang-glider?

Otto Lilienthal, a German engineer, designed and flew over 15 different hang-gliders. He made the first flight in which the pilot controlled the machine. Lilienthal died in 1896 when his hang-glider crashed.

Who were the Wright brothers?

The American brothers Orville and Wilbur Wright had the idea of fitting a petrol engine and propeller to their glider. On 17 December 1903, Orville made the world's first powered flight. *Flyer 1* flew for 12 seconds and covered 37 metres – less than the length of a jumbo jet!

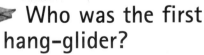

How do helicopters rise up vertically?

Helicopters have one or two large rotors made up of long, thin wings. When the rotors spin round, they lift the aircraft and drive it along. Helicopters can fly forwards, backwards and sideways. The first single-blade helicopter was built by Russian-American Sikorsky in 1939.

Can aeroplanes land by themselves?

Modern jet liners are controlled from a hi-tech flight deck. They even have computer-controlled autopilot systems to land planes in bad weather when the pilot cannot see the runway clearly. The first autopilot landing of a scheduled airliner was in 1965 at Heathrow Airport, England.

What were zeppelins?

Zeppelins, named after their German inventor Ferdinand von Zeppelin, were giant airships up to 240 metres in length. They were powered by petrol engines and a propeller, and filled with hydrogen gas which is lighter than air but very flammable. The first zeppelin flight was in 1900.

Are helicopters really 500 years old?

The Italian artist and inventor Leonardo da Vinci sketched a simple helicopter (see above) over 500 years ago, but it was never built. The French inventor Paul Cornu built the first helicopter in 1907 – it rose to a height of 30 centimetres and hovered there for 20 seconds. Cornu's helicopter was very difficult to control, and it was not until the 1930s that helicopters became a practical means of flying.

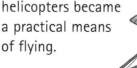

Jet power – when and where?

Gloster E28/39 jet

In the 1930s, both Britain and Germany were working on a new form of power for aircraft – the jet engine. The British engineer Frank Whittle came up with the idea in 1929, and prototypes were built by Whittle in Britain and by Hans von Ohain in Germany. The first jet aircraft, built by the German Ernst Heinkel, took to the air in 1939. Two years later, Whittle's engine powered the *Gloster* E28/39 jet. Jet engines allow planes to travel much faster – some military jets can zoom along at 3,200 kilometres an hour!

Quick-fire Quiz

1. Name the Wright brothers' first plane:
a) *Gloster*
b) *Flyer 1*
c) *Orville*

2. Who was the first hang-glider pilot?
a) Zeppelin
b) Whittle
c) Lilienthal

3. Which gas was used in zeppelins?
a) Oxygen
b) Air
c) Hydrogen

4. Who sketched the first helicopter?
a) George Cayley
b) Montgolfier brothers
c) Leonardo da Vinci

Into Space

In the early 1950s, the United States and Soviet Union began the space race. In 1957 the Russians launched the first satellite, *Sputnik I*. Four years later, the Russian cosmonaut Yuri Gagarin blasted into orbit in *Vostock I*. His historic trip round the world lasted for under 2 hours, but manned space flight was launched.

Who first saw stars?

In 1609, the Italian scientist Galileo was the first person to look at the stars through a telescope. His studies led him to suggest that the Earth moved round the Sun and was not at the centre of the Universe as people then thought.

Why do telescopes detect radio waves?

Stars and other objects in space give out radio waves as well as light. Radio telescopes have huge dish-shaped antennae to pick up these radio waves. Radio telescopes have discovered exploding galaxies, radiation from distant galaxies and spinning neutron stars called pulsars.

Is there life on other planets?

The other planets in our Solar System are probably not able to support life, but scientists are looking further afield. In 1974, astronomers beamed a radio message out into space from a huge radio telescope in Puerto Rico. They aimed it at a dense star cluster, M13, over 25,000 light years away. The message is travelling at the speed of light so we will have to wait 50,000 years for a reply!

Mariner 9

What is a space probe?

Space probes are unmanned spacecraft that travel into space. Several have been sent to other planets in the Solar System. *Mariner 9*, launched in 1971, visited Mars. *Mariner 10*, launched in 1973, was the first probe to visit two planets. It flew by Venus and visited Mercury three times, where it found that the daytime temperatures were hot enough to melt lead.

Who was the first man on the Moon?

The American Neil Armstrong was the first man to set foot on the Moon in July 1969. He and fellow astronaut Edwin 'Buzz' Aldrin put up the American flag and a plaque saying 'We come in peace for all mankind'.

When did people first walk in space?

In 1965, the Russian Aleksei Leonov made the first space walk, but he had to remain attached to the spacecraft. In the early 1980s, scientists developed the MMU (manned manoeuvring unit), which let astronauts walk freely in space. The first free space walk took place from the American *Challenger* in 1984.

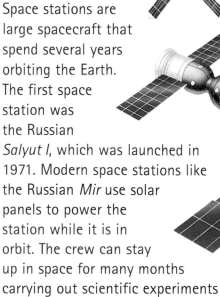

What is a shuttle?

Early spacecraft used rocket power to blast them into space. Then the Americans came up with the idea of building a re-usable spacecraft. The shuttle still needs rocket power to take off, but it lands like an aircraft and so can be re-used. In 1981, the first space shuttle, *Columbia*, took off.

What is a space station?

Space stations are large spacecraft that spend several years orbiting the Earth. The first space station was the Russian *Salyut I*, which was launched in 1971. Modern space stations like the Russian *Mir* use solar panels to power the station while it is in orbit. The crew can stay up in space for many months carrying out scientific experiments and repairing equipment.

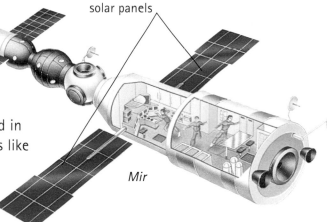

solar panels

Mir

Timeline

Hundreds of inventions and discoveries have marked human progress from the Stone Age to the Space Age. Some happened by accident, others took people years to perfect. Here are a few important milestones.

20000 BC to 2000 BC

c.20000 BC Bone needles used
c.8000 BC First permanent houses built
4000–3000 BC Earliest known writing (cuneiform) (Sumeria)
3500 BC Simple ploughs pulled by people (Sumeria)
3200 BC About 300 years after the potter's wheel was invented, people made simple wheeled vehicles (Sumeria)
3000 BC Simple glass beads made (Egypt)
c.2800 BC Stonehenge built in England; first step pyramids built in Egypt
2350 BC First lavatories with pedestals (Mesopotamia)

1900 BC to 0

c.1900 BC Metal workers began extracting iron from its ore; steel was made c.1200 BC
1000–700 First shadow clocks (Egypt); by 700 BC divided sundial was in use
c.690 BC First bridges (aqueducts) used to carry water (Assyria)
c.620 BC First coins made from electrum in Lydia (Asia Minor)
c.450 BC Decimal abacus c.450 BC; early stick and dust tray abacus (Mesopotamia c.2500 BC)
c.85 BC First water-powered mills used to grind flour (Greece)

AD 1 to 1400

105 Tsai Lun made paper from pulp (China)
600 Chess developed (India or China)
c.840 Camera obscura developed (China)
c.868 First printed book *Diamond Sutra* (China)
c.1000 Spinning wheel used (Asia)
c.1090 Magnetic compass invented (China, Arabia)
c.1300 First mechanical clocks with equal time periods developed (Europe)
c.1300 Astrolabe adapted for sea navigation (Arabia)

1401 to 1700

c.1440 Johannes Gutenberg developed printing press with movable type (Germany); first book printed c.1450
c.1590 Janssen made compound microscope (Netherlands)
c.1592 Galileo made first thermometer (Italy)
1608 Hans Lippershey made working telescope (Netherlands)
1609 Galileo first person to look at stars (Italy)
c. 1620 Drebble built first submarine (England)
c. 1642 Pascal built calculating machine (France)
c.1683 Antonie van Leeuwenhoek made first high-power (x 200) microscope (Netherlands)

1701 to 1800

1712 Newcomen built steam-powered engine (England)
1714 Fahrenheit developed mercury thermometer (Germany)
1752 Franklin developed lightning conductor (USA)
1757 John Campbell built sextant (England)
1759 Harrison developed accurate chronometer (England)
1764 James Hargreaves built spinning jenny (England)
1765 Watt built condensing steam engine (Scotland)
1769 Richard Arkwright built powered spinning machine (England)
1783 Montgolfier brothers built first practical hot-air balloon (France)
1783 Jouffroy D'Abbans built first steam boat (France)
1785 Cartwright built power loom (England)

1801 to 1900

1803 Richard Trevethick built steam train (England)
1821 Michael Faraday made first electric motor (England)
c.1827 First photograph taken by Niépce (France)
1829 Stevenson's steam train *Rocket* was
built (England)
1829 Sewing machine built by Thimonnier
(France)
1837 Telegraph developed by Morse (USA)
and Cooke and Wheatstone (England)
1839 First practical bicycle built by
Kirkpatrick Macmillan (Scotland)
1852 Henri Gifford built first working (steam-powered)
airship (France)
1853 George Cayley pioneered glider technology
(England)
1856 Henry Bessemer invented cheap steel-making
process (England)
1865 Lister first used antiseptics (England)
1867 Joseph Monier developed wire-
reinforced concrete (France)
1873 C. L. Sholes made first
practical commercial typewriter
(USA) (went on sale in 1874)
1875 Scot Alexander Graham
Bell invented telephone (USA)
1877 Thomas Edison developed
the phonograph (USA)
1878/9 Swan (England) and
Edison (USA) made electric light bulb
1882 First power station opened by
Edison (USA)
1882 Henry Seely built first practical electric iron (USA)
1884 Gottlieb Daimler made first light-weight petrol
engines (Germany)
1885 Karl Benz made first petrol-driven motor car
(Germany)
1893 W. Judson made the first slide fastener
(USA)
1895 Wilhelm Röntgen discovered
X-rays (Germany)
1895 Marconi invented radio
communication (Italy)
1895 Auguste and Louis Lumière first
showed a 'movie' to an audience
(France)

1901 to 2000

1903 Wright brothers flew first powered aircraft (USA)
1907 First helicopter built by Paul Cornu (France)
1925 John Logie Baird invented television and
demonstrated it in 1926 (Scotland)
1929 Whittle patented idea of the jet
engine (England)
1933 Polythene discovered at ICI (England)
1935 Wallace Carothers made nylon (USA)
1936 Focke made first practical helicopter
(Germany)
1942 Enrico Fermi built first nuclear
reactor (USA)
1945 Mauchly and Eckert developed first proper computer
(USA)
1947 Edwin Land invented polaroid camera (USA)
1948 First atomic clock built (USA)
1953 DNA double-helix discovered by F. Crick (England),
J Watson (USA) and M. Wilkins (England)
1955 Cockerel invented hovercraft (England)
1957 First artificial Earth satellite went into orbit (USSR)
1959 Integrated circuit (silicon chip) developed (USA)
1960 T. Maiman developed laser (USA)
1961 First manned space flight (Russia)
1964 Computer mouse invented by Engelhart (USA)
1967 First heart transplant by C. Barnard (South Africa)
1969 First manned moon landing (USA)
1970 Floppy disk developed by IBM (USA)
1971 Microprocessor patented by Intel (USA)
1978 Successful PC developed by Jobs and Wozniak (USA)
1979 Compact disk developed by Sony and Philips
1981 Space shuttle developed (USA)
1983 Satellite TV developed (USA)
1984 Genetic fingerprinting developed (Britain)
1989 Game Boy™ launched by Nintendo (Japan)
c1992 Virtual reality helmets devised (USA)
1992 First map of human chromosome
(France, Britain, USA)
1994 Longest undersea tunnel, 50km-long
Channel Tunnel opens (Britain, France)
1995 First DNA database set up (Britain)
1997 First successful clone of a mammal
(Britain)
c.1997 Sikorsky developed robotic helicopter (USA)
1997 Biorobotics pioneered by Shimoyama's
team (Japan)

Index

abacus 22
advertisement 5
aircraft 33, 34, 35
antiseptics 7
aqualung 32
aqueduct 8
artificial limbs 7
astrolabe 22
astronauts 36, 37
atomic energy 21

bacteria 6
Bakelite 17
ball games 18, 19
ballpoint pen (biro) 5
blood flow 6
board games 18, 19
bridges 8, 9
buildings 8–9, 12, 13

calculator 22, 23, 25
camcorder 29
camera 28, 29
car 30, 31
central heating 13
china (porcelain) 17
chronometer 32
cinema (movies) 28, 29
clocks 23
clones (animal) 11
clothes 14, 15
combine harvester 10
compact disks (CDs) 25
computer 5, 24, 25, 35

deoxyribonucleic acid (DNA) 7
diving bell 32
drugs (medicines) 6

electricity 12, 13, 20, 21
energy 20–21
engines 30, 31, 32, 34

factories 15, 20
farms 10, 11, 15
farm machinery 10, 11
felt-tip pen 5
fertilizers 10
fibreglass 16, 17
furniture 12

games 18, 19
glass 16, 26, 27

hang-glider 34
helicopter 35
hieroglyphs 5
hot-air balloon 34
hovercraft 33
hypocaust 13

insecticides 11
Internet 25
iron (electric) 12

jet engine 35

kite 33

laser 25
latitude 22, 32
leather 15
light bulb 13

longitude 22, 32
loom 14

measurements 22, 23
medicine 6–7
microscope 6
microwave oven 13
milking machine 10
money 22
Morse Code 27

navigation 22, 32
needles 14
numbers 22, 23, 25
nylon 16, 17

oil 21
Olympic games 19
optical fibres 26

paper clip 4
papyrus 5
pencil 5
pesticide 11
photography 28, 29
plastics 16, 17
plough 10
power stations 21
printing press 4, 26
pyramids 9

radio 27
radio telescope 36
refrigerator 12
robots 25
rubber 17

satellites (artificial) 27, 36
seed drill 11
sewing machine 15
ships 32, 33
shoes 15
silk 15
skyscrapers 8, 9
solar power 21, 31
space flight 36, 37
spinning jenny 15
steam engines 20, 30, 31, 32
steel 16
submarine 33

telegraph 27
telephone 26, 27
telescopes 36
television 28, 29
thermometer 23
toilet 13
toys 18, 19
trains 30, 31
typewriter 4

Velcro 15
video games 19
virtual reality 25

weights 22
wheel 30
windmills 10, 20
writing 4

X-rays 7

zip fastener 14

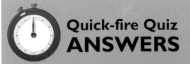

Quick-fire Quiz ANSWERS

Page 5 Writing and Printing
1. a   2. c   3. c   4. b

Page 7 Medicine
1. c   2. b   3. a   4. c

Page 9 Buildings
1. c   2. b   3. b   4. c

Page 11 Food and Agriculture
1. b   2. c   3. a   4. b

Page 13 At Home
1. c   2. b   3. a   4. b

Page 15 Clothes and Fabric
1. c   2. c   3. c   4. a

Page 17 Useful Materials
1. b   2. c   3. b   4. a

Page 19 Toys and Games
1. b   2. a   3. b   4. c

Page 21 Energy
1. b   2. c   3. a   4. c

Page 23 Calculations
1. b   2. c   3. b   4. b

Page 25 Computers
1. b   2. c   3. a   4. c

Page 27 Communication
1. b   2. c   3. b   4. b

Page 29 On Film
1. b   2. c   3. a   4. c

Page 31 Travel on Land
1. b   2. b   3. c   4. b

Page 33 On the Sea
1. b   2. b   3. c   4. c

Page 35 By Air
1. b   2. c   3. c   4. c

Page 37 Into Space
1. c   2. b   3. c   4. b